Every Drop of Rain

A Poet's Way Through Grief

By Katherine Niebur
• 2009

To Gretchen—
Some journeys
are hard, but
not travelled alone—

Kate Niebur
2-19-2020

About the Author

Katherine Niebur graduated from San Diego State University in 1992 with a degree in Business Administration (Information Systems). She is currently a computer careers instructor at a local technical college. She has two children, three step-children, four grandchildren and lives in Hastings, Minnesota where she enjoys her hobbies of gardening and writing poetry. Katherine is available for public speaking and poetry readings and can be contacted via her website at www.apoetsway.com.

Visit www.booksurge.com or www.apoetsway.com to order additional copies

Dedication

This book is dedicated to my husband
Thomas John Niebur
June 5, 1948 – August 23, 2005

We carry you forward,
because we couldn't possibly
leave you behind.

Acknowledgements

To Luke and Ashley because we have shared this journey and survived.

To the doctors and care-givers at the Mayo Clinic who tried so valiantly to save my husband's life.

To the Niebur's and the Nicolai's for keeping me in their family.

To Catherine Virca for her many personal sacrifices to stay by my side in the darkest of times, and to Nick, for sharing her so generously.

To Valerie DeRosch for her initial editing and feedback on this manuscript and whose encouragement kept the project alive.

To the rest of the GF's whose collective warmth and wisdom has been my security blanket for years.

To Doug Verboult for helping me make all those birdhouses!

To Mark Niebur for clearing the way for the memorial garden.

To the grief support group in Hastings, MN and all who participate there to lift grief survivors from their despair. Special thanks to Marty, Lyla and Judy for their love and support and to Richard Close for inspiring the first poem "Bringing You Forward".

Special Acknowledgement

to the Mayo Clinic in Rochester, MN

The miracle of the Mayo clinic
may not be as much in their ability to cure,
as in their ability to care.

With gratitude,

Katherine Niebur

Foreword

If you have walked a loved one through cancer, you understand the rollercoaster ride of hope and hopelessness, of courage and fear. If you have experienced the loss of a loving partner, you understand the rotating shock, denial, anger, sadness, loneliness, depression and despair that become companions in the daily experience of grief. It is very difficult to describe the feelings to anyone else. The loss leaves a gaping hole in your life and you wander around for a time in that huge space, encountering pain and emotions you never knew existed.

Everyone grieves differently. I turned to writing, trying to express the emotions tumbling within. When I began to see that poetry, with its economy of words, could draw out the deepest pockets of pain and lay them on the pages, I began to feel relief. Then, as I shared the poems with others, I could see they provoked the emotional responses, not just the intellectual understanding but also the actual emotional understanding of what I was trying to describe. That's when I began to think the poetry might help other people.

Those who have traveled this road will recognize its landmarks in these poems, including the frustration of fighting and losing to cancer, the suicidal thoughts and death wishes that can accompany early grief, the despair, the questioning of God and meaning, the altered perspective on what it is to live and the ultimate incorporation of the loss into your personal history. I hope the words describe at least a portion of your experience; if they make you weep, I think they are good tears.

For those of you who have not yet personally traveled this road, I hope the words help you understand a little more about friends and loved ones who are on the grief journey.

These are my hopes in publishing "Every Drop of Rain".

- Katherine Niebur, 2008

Contents

Battling Cancer

Battling Cancer

My husband, then my fiancé, was diagnosed with an aggressive form of lymphoma in early 2004. From that point, we spent months walking the corridors of the Mayo Clinic in Rochester, Minnesota, with our orders in hand, going from station to station for test after test, treatment after treatment. Sometimes, the news was good and our hopes were high; sometimes, the news was bad and we were afraid; most times, we were in a kind of blessed denial.

The Mayo Clinic is beautiful and made more so by the art, sculptures and gardens within and around the buildings. It creates a kind of surreal experience when you wander with the sick, surrounded by the serenity. We met many other cancer patients and their families, all heroic, fighting an internal enemy with the weapons of medicine, prayer and hope. Many times, we felt so much luckier than others we met. Our treatment results seemed so positive, Tom was so strong and we had the loving support of a wonderful circle of family and friends. While we traveled only 50 miles to the Mayo Clinic and faced cancer together, many traveled from around the world and, separated from loved ones, fought the battle alone. The children with cancer especially tugged at our hearts. Sitting across from a child as tubes to deliver chemo therapy were inserted into the ports in their tiny chests, our burdens seemed non-existent. Their courage was humbling and inspiring.

The roles of those involved in the cancer battle seem to fall into place. The patient is positive, determined, stoic and seems to want to comfort others more than be comforted. The oncologists are cautiously optimistic when they can be, but careful to make no promises. The oncology nurses have seen it all, those they thought would die but survived and those they thought would survive but died. They seem to have developed an 'anything can happen' attitude and having no reason to expect the worst, they stay steadfastly positive and optimistic – they are truly the greatest givers of hope.

For the caregiver, it is the ultimate balancing act. Every bit of information given by the doctors is analyzed – both what is said and what is unsaid. The patient may not hear or not be willing to hear what is laid between the lines. If the caregiver lets on, lets down completely into their own reactions, they are not doing their self-appointed job of holding their loved one up – and there is a kind of creeping irrational fear that if they show any worry they may somehow be complicit in their loved-one's decline. The lines between faith, hope, wishes and superstition can become very gray. I don't think I'm the only caregiver who ever thought at times, "If I stay positive, he'll live" and its counterpart, "If I show fear, he'll die." We can be so cruel to ourselves sometimes.

As the primary messenger to friends and family I wanted to tell enough to keep everyone informed but never more than Tom wanted me to – serious illness is a very personal battle and your loved-one deserves to decide who will know what, and when. I don't think I'm the only such messenger who wrote and rewrote a status email, struggling to find the right mix of optimism and realism.

In the process of fighting the illness, I built a kind of scaffolding to support myself and everyone else. I prioritized tasks, scheduled caregivers for times I had to be at work and found strength I didn't know I had. I propped up everything with quick, necessary decisions, praying they were the right ones. I lived solidly in the expectation the situation was temporary and although I didn't know how long my 'scaffolding' would have to hold, I knew it would just be temporary and everything would be o.k. in the end. I lived in the expectation that Tom would live. The alternative seemed unthinkable.

The Diagnosis

Cancer, not bronchitis
Cancer, not pneumonia
Cancer, not pleurisy
Cancer, not a virus

Cancer

We sat dumb
Staring at the doctor
Absorbing the reality
Reaching into the disbelief
For the handle of courage
To brace ourselves
For all that came next

~ K. Niebur

They had to name it
to treat it…
but it was an unknown.
Some kind of
Non-Hodgkins Lymphoma
'Burkitt's-like'
and
aggressive…

Treatment

Sitting slumped in chairs
Apparently dozing…
A wiggling foot
A shift, a sigh
Betraying our impatience
Staring out and in…
Waiting and more waiting

Finally a diagnosis of type and stage
Not good
And a treatment plan
The Vanderbilt method
A most aggressive intervention
For a most aggressive cancer

I stood by helplessly as they
Told my fiancé the drugs to save him
Could also kill him…

Then the nurse parade began
Hanging bag after bag of medication
This one to shield his kidneys
That one to flush the cancer
("Did you know, that you actually
pee away your dead cancer cells?",
"No, I didn't know that.
Didn't really ever want to know that.")

The machines churning and churning
as they pumped the chemo into his veins

Their rhythm broken only
by their punishing beep
Chirping for the next bag…

The first night was hushed
as I tenderly helped him
with tasks so achingly private
Clumsy and terrified
trying to be competent
How I ached for this man's man
who found it so hard to be helpless
he clenched his jaw
to keep from pushing my hands away

Later in the night
sleeping on a cot beside him
the machine sounds worked their way
into my dreams and turned them into nightmares
It was I who woke screaming
while he dozed peacefully, peacefully
dreaming only of God

~ K. Niebur

The Exhale

One and a half rounds
of chemo done
Awaiting again the tests
Draining of blood
and spinal fluid
MRI's and scans

Tensely waiting
in doctor's chambers
Watching the minute hand
Willing it forward
Willing
it
forward...

Finally, finally
the door opens
The doctor arrives
Greetings are made
I scan his face for a tell
that never shows
Such masters, these oncologists
They must win every hand
of poker they play

The good news finally comes...
The cancer is on the run
We are winning, winning
the battle and maybe the war...

We don't look at each other
We can neither laugh nor cry
We look down, as if in prayer
and exhale in unison…
… Thank God
… Thank God
Thanks be to God

~K. Niebur

Going Home I

On that freeway journey home
the scenery didn't blend
From speed, day dreams or teary eyes
as we discussed the end

The sunshine tumbled on the miles
as if to light the way
We dared to hope and plan again
in terms of years, not days

The hard times lifted in that glow
Blown 'way like leaves on wind
We watched them floating far away
Bid goodbye and good end

~K. Niebur

After more chemo therapy
and a stem-cell transplant
he was hairless and weak
and we waited for the verdict...

Just One Spot

The doctor squinted at the screen
flipped images and scans
Back and forth and left and right
mouse racing in his hand

He stopped and studied, pursed his lips
then forced his frown away
Turned with hand upon his hip
We braced for what he'd say

"There's just this one small spot", he said
"and PET scans tend to lie.
They see too much but not enough
to count on; to rely.

The spot's too small to prod or poke,
to biopsy, remove.
It would only make us question more
than we could ever prove.

Radiation brings its risks
and surgery's not wise
Immunities are down and weak..
Your system's compromised

The choice is yours, not mine to say.
We could wait it out and see.
I'd tend to give you passing grades
Declare you cancer free."

~ K.Niebur

"Cancer-free"
But......?

Going Home 2

Now we travel home again
In silence
Lost in thought
Punctuated by hope
Fueled by denial

The spot, that spot
What does it mean?
Nothing or something?
Nothing or everything?

We take turns finding hope
We take turns fighting despair
We take turns faking joy

Surely, God won't let us down
Won't let us come this close
Won't let us fight this long and hard
Won't disregard all the prayers
of family and friends
the prayers
of people we don't even know

Surely,
We will have our miracle!
Our story will have a happy ending
To be told and then re-told
We decide to count on life
And let the rest unfold

~K. Niebur

How much of life do you delay
when hours must take the place
of days...?

We Married, Anyway

We talked about our former plans
to marry...perhaps...some day
With each moment, now so full
that seemed too far away

In those moments spent together
Clinging to hope and faith
All former doubts just shed away
And love took hold its place

We knew our future was a guess
And life could fly away
Uncertain of all tomorrows
We married, anyway

~ K.Niebur

We knew it wasn't good…
but we thought
there would be
more…
some new treatment
some trial
some miracle…

A Single Tear

Waiting in the room again
he sits stoically
on the naugahide couch,
Weak from treatment and transfusions
while I wander and pace
Examining pictures and degrees,
Thumbing thru the Doctor's journals,
Looking for the article that says
"Cure for Cancer"
Surely, they just missed it…

Finally, finally
The door opens, again
The doctor arrives, again
Greetings are made, again
I scan her face, again

But this time,
I see…
a single tear

~K. Niebur

Saying Goodbye

Saying Goodbye

Finally, when we were told there was nothing more they could do – no more treatments – no medical miracles – no experimental treatment – nothing left but to make him comfortable – we let go of the fight and prepared for his death.

He wanted to die at home. We made hospice care arrangements. I learned to administer his pain medication, arranged for family members to be with him 24/7, and somehow got the final preparations made for the courses I had to teach in the Fall. We thought we would have a few weeks together but he declined in days.

The house was so full of people and as my husband struggled to breathe, I was afraid he would die before I could tell him, in private, how much he meant to me. So, one afternoon, I leaned down and whispered my goodbye in his ear, so no one else could hear. Afterwards, he became still as glass. I knew my words had touched him and I imagined he was trying so hard to reach down into his dying to find the strength to respond. His fingers moved slightly in my hand. I kissed away his struggle and told him to rest. I knew what was in his heart at that moment.

Your Silence Spoke

And in the end you could not speak
to tell me what you'd need
I questioned you and listened close
to every sound you breathed

As you slipped on I knew I had
to make sure that you knew
I never knew a man so fine
So wonderful as you

I leaned down and placed my cheek
against your pallid skin
to whisper words you had to hear
unsure where to begin

"You're the most enlightened man," I said,
"I have ever known…
God bless you on your journey now;
Go when you need to go.

And thank you for allowing me
to love you all this time."
I know you heard because I felt
your hand move soft in mine

"I love you, too." you couldn't say
Though I could see you try
Your struggle broke my heart in two
And gave me your reply

K. Niebur

I insisted I still felt his pulse...
but a voice behind me said quietly
"He's gone...he's gone"
and he was.

Last Breath

I touched my forehead
...to your chest
I whispered out your name...
...again and again in disbelief...
...a chant of unbound pain

I knew...I knew...
...I had no right
...to beg you stay with me

I kissed your soul as it took flight
...and sadly set you free

~ K. Niebur

The Funeral

The Funeral

At the funeral, I was coping outwardly, the way many widows do. There is a kind of numbness that comes over you so you can make it through the event. You operate on automatic pilot – like a trauma victim, which you are. Only later, when things are quiet and you are alone do your feelings begin to return, and it is simply an overwhelming flood of pain.

Wakes and funerals...
They help us say goodbye....
but it can be torment
for the family...

The Funeral

At first, it's like a vice so tight
Your heart can't feel a thing
Just stand through hours of shaking hands
Sit mute through hymns they sing

Then walk the casket out the door
Down steps into the rain
Leave one last kiss on coffin's wood
Sleep-walk back in again

Stand in line and dish the food
the volunteers prepared
Sit and eat and drink and talk
Words spinning in the air

Go home and sit
'till someone guides you to the bed you shared
Tucks you in and leaves you safe
to mend by sleep's repair

And then the vice starts loosening
so slow no one can see
The agony pours in and in
like tidal wave from sea

You beg your God to take your life
Would suicide be fair?
What heavenly judge could call it sin
to end the pain you bear?

The only thing that holds you back
is just the guilty fear
That should you die by your own hand,
you'd never join him there

Where in God's care, he's feeling fine
Quite happy without you
So you go on; you just don't know
what else is left to do

~ K. Niebur

The Space Left Behind

The Space Left Behind

There is a huge space left behind when someone that close to you dies. It is an emptiness like no other and the physical sense of it is stunning. How is it that this space they leave behind is so very much bigger than the space they physically occupied? It is as if the laws of physics, of volume are as broken as your heart. You still expect to see them come walking through the door.

And when the pain comes into this void, there is no buffer. It is pure, deep and ravaging. I kept telling myself that others had survived this so it had to be possible. Still, I often wished I could simply make myself stop breathing. I wished I could walk into the woods, sit down and die. I had heard somewhere of a custom where the widow throws herself on the funeral pyre to burn up with her husband, and I thought now, I understood why.

And where does everybody go? Your scaffolding has crumbled and you are abandoned in the rubble. All those friends and family are gone away to process their own grief. They don't know how to help you or what to say. Your pain is so palpable that being in your presence is sometimes just too painful for them. They love you and tell you to call if you need anything. But you are paralyzed by that pain and your hand can't reach the phone. Besides, it's 2 or 3 a.m. when you need someone the most, not some time that is convenient for anyone else. And so, you are alone for the worst of it.

I kept expecting him
to just..come home..

Denial

I look for you in every room
You must be here, I still need you
You've never let me down before
I'll just wait here and watch the door

~K. Niebur

Time passes...
but it doesn't feel healing, at first...

Time does not Heal

These days, these nights blur by like trains
These prayers, these pleas, this endless pain
There's no one in this void with me
No one but you, which cannot be

These seconds, they just won't tick by
They linger, lie, and make me cry
Time does not heal, it drags the pain
Along behind bound up in chain

I'm not sure if it's dawn or dusk
Just know that I still think of us
On the brink of future dreams
With all the time we'd ever need

I begged you in the dark last night
My darling, lost one, bring the light
Don't leave me here to drift alone
Guide me, guide me, guide me home

~K. Niebur

And space changes…
It feels so much bigger…

The Space Left Behind

I saw you die; I buried you.
I packed away your empty clothes
So they wouldn't remind me
I hid your shoes and hats and gloves
So they wouldn't haunt me
I piled pillows and books
Magazines and newspapers
On your side of the bed
So I wouldn't feel alone
I kept routines and invented new ones
So I wouldn't get lost without you

And when I had done all that
I sat and tried to understand
Just *where* you had gone
Where ?

Then…
I simply floated..
for days and days..
In the vastness of the space
You left behind

~K.Niebur

Just a Little More Time

Just a Little More Time

Tom left behind a son, then 16, and a daughter on the brink of her 21st birthday. We all spoke of our longing for 'just a little more time'. But I have sat next to widows who had decades with their husbands, and it is never enough time.

No matter what…
we just don't expect this.

I Didn't Know

I thought I'd have more time with you
More time to let you know
How very much you meant to me
It didn't always show

I hurried out the door each day
Without a single care
I knew that when my day was done
You'd still be waiting there

I'd breeze back in and say hello
We'd talk about our day
Small news, big news all aired out
No lack of things to say

I rarely stopped the idle flow
To really look and see
The loving soul behind your eyes
So much amused by me

I never gave much thought, you see
To endings come too soon
And now I come back home at night
To dark and empty rooms

~ K. Niebur

How do you comfort
a grieving son...
once, so full of joy...

Just one more hug
(For Luke)

"I just want one more hug", he cried
"Just one more chance to know
The warmth and comfort of his arms
Now I've no place to go

No one can give me refuge now
And the world's too big for me
When I was hurt or mad or scared
He always came to me

Dad talked to me and held me close
And I could let tears flow
I needed him and need him still
Why did he have to go"?

I took your son into my arms
Asked God to still my fears
Help me help him, Lord, I prayed
Then I just shared his tears

~ K. Niebur

How do you reach
a grieving daughter...
once, so full of dreams

Once More

I wish once more
I could see his living flesh
His chest rising as he took a breath
If only I could hear his voice
Advice I could always use
Laughter about almost anything
Shouting for the Vikings,
"Get him! GET HIM!"

His prayers,
not only for himself,
but for everyone else
Once more, I want to touch his warm skin
Hold his hand in church
Comb my hand through his soft hair
Hug him so tight
Tell him I love him
Once again,
to say
"Good night"
I miss you, I love you, don't forget me.
I love you dad.

~ Ashley Niebur

Everything would be ok...
If we could just talk to you...

To Talk to You

I had a terrible day, today
Doing chores you used to do
I didn't know how to do them right
And I wanted to talk to you

The day before at work
I felt the need, then, too
I reached for the phone instinctively
I wanted to talk to you

Last week I had decisions to make
and taxes coming due
I figured it out and juggled the funds
But I wanted to talk to you

Last night, a fear surrounded me
A loneliness so huge
I tried to think of who to call
But I wanted to talk to you

You always knew just what to say
And always what to do
That's who you'll always be for us
And we want to talk to you

~ K. Niebur

I guess it was just...
too much to ask...

All I Want

All I want is not so much.
To see his face and feel his touch
To have him back with me again
My love, my life, my truest friend

All I want? A few more years
Of life and love, of joy and tears
About a hundred more would do
Give or take just one or two

All I want? For him to hear
His grandchild's song, so sweet and dear
To see him melt and watch his frown
Transform until it's upside down

All I want? To lose all time
To fade and hold his hand in mine
To grow so old we both forget
Just when and where and how we met

All I want? To share our death
To hear each other's last soft breath
To cross beyond God's garden gate
And meet as one, our final fate

~K. Niebur

Aching

Aching

There is a period of time when the sharpness of the pain gives way to the deeper ache of grieving and the best you can do is surrender to it.

If I could just figure out
when the grief is the hardest...
maybe I could manage it...

I Only Grieve When...

I only grieve when I first wake
And strain to hear the sound
Of shower flow or dresser drawers
Bang shut as you move 'round

I only grieve when I come home
And you're not standing there
Or sitting where you used to be
To reach and stroke my hair

I only grieve when I don't hear
Your voice so low, so strong
Not saying much but speaking truths
That I so counted on

I only grieve when nighttime comes
And sleeplessness begins
I only grieve when I breathe out
And when I breathe back in

~K. Niebur

I still feel you…

Camelot

I cannot stop the tears tonight
They trail down on my face
Drip freely on the novel's page
To stain and mark my place

I sigh and close the book again
Can't follow any plot
That doesn't tell of you and me
In our sweet Camelot

I almost feel you touch my skin
Your lips brush soft on mine
Our passion so intense and free
Crescendos so sublime

I douse the light and close my eyes
But sleep won't come to me
I reach across to take your hand
And breach eternity

~K. Niebur

Will this ever go away...?

Still Crying

Every day, it seems
The tears come again
They surprise me with their wet anger
And utter desperation

One would think such tears
Would dry forever
when the soul
is finally drained
of all understanding
and all hope

But grief is a well
With no measurable depth
A sound that echoes forever
An invisible wound
Weeping beneath its scar
And slow, so slow to heal

~K. Niebur

Regret

Regret

I don't think it is possible to lose someone so tragically without experiencing an internal tirade of 'if only's'. If only the cancer had been more accurately diagnosed; if only the transplant had worked; if only we had insisted on radiation; if only we had more time; if only I had prayed more…if only..

And once your loved one is gone, you have plenty of time to examine past failures. I wish I had helped you more with chores; I wish I had made you stop for more sunsets; I wish I had talked much less and listened much more…I wish…

Was my faith not strong enough?

I Didn't Pray Enough

All those times in Mayo's halls
I wandered round and round
I should have stayed down on my knees
Much closer to the ground

Had I only prayed the perfect words
Your life would have been spared
I should have stayed put at the Cross
Instead of running scared

I prayed and prayed then walked and walked
Running from my fears
I should have stayed down on my knees
Then, you'd still be here

~ K. Niebur

Was I just not smart enough?

I'm Sorry

I'm sorry for small unkindnesses
For things I sometimes said
I'm sorry I made you turn down the TV
Each night we went to bed

I'm sorry I didn't understand
How hard you worked for us
I'm sorry for every single complaint
Each time I made a fuss

I'm sorry for times I failed to be
A better friend and wife
And sorry, my darling, so sorry forever
I couldn't save your life

~ K. Niebur

Questioning God

Questioning God

When grieving, many people go through a period of questioning their faith. How could God let this happen? Why, when my husband's treatment was supposed to be nearly 90% successful, did he have to be in the 10% who died anyway? Why do others get to live, while he had to die? Why?

I had to stop going to church for a time because when I sat down in the pew my sadness sank down so deeply in my heart, I would begin weeping. I might have done fine during the week, but when I got to church where I automatically surrendered all my defenses at the door, the silent tears would just pour down my face. I knew I wasn't supposed to be embarrassed to cry in God's house but I was embarrassed to cry around the people in the pews beside me, in front of me…I was embarrassed to take my tear-stained face down the aisle for communion. I didn't want to draw attention – or pity. Sometimes the sadness would descend before I even arrived at church, the tears would start falling and I would simply turn my car around and drive home to grieve and pray in private.

I never stopped believing in God, but I had so many, many unanswered questions.

Maybe if I prayed...
for what I really, really
want...

Just Give Him Back to Me

Today I gave up all pretense
All dignity and common sense
I fell down on my bended knees
And prayed "Just give him back to me."

"Turn back time and change the end
Make him whole and live again
Make him cured and make him strong
Send him back where he belongs

You have the power to make it so
And no one ever has to know
Make it so we can't recall
We ever said goodbye at all

I'll close my eyes so I won't see
The way you bring this all to be
Show your mercy on me, please
I pray, just give him back to me"

~K. Niebur

People always say this...
Why?

The Better Place

They say you're in a better place
But what place would that be
That wouldn't let me touch your face
And keep you near to me?

How can it be a loving God
Lets hearts grow so entwined
Then calls one on to the better place
While leaving one behind?

What bigger plan is playing on
What lesson, reason, rhyme
Take one of us to the better place
Leaves one, so lost, behind?

Why let us join that deep and true
Why let our roots combine
Then pluck one up to the better place
Leave one to wilt behind?

There must be some kind of mistake
God erred just this one time
There just can't be a better place
You can't be in a better place
You'd never want a better place
Without your hand in mine

~K. Niebur

Perspective and Hope

Perspective and Hope

This experience alters you forever and you know it. There is simply a profound distinction between your self before the death and your self after the death. Things that once mattered seem almost amusing, our own death does not seem so frightening, and things once taken for granted are treasured with much greater awareness.

He spins us down to earth..
...then brings us home at will

It's not funny

I know it isn't funny
When friends I hold so dear
Are plotting, planning all the ways
To last another year

They count the carbs and trim the fat
Detoxify, deprive
They run and walk and bike and hike
And try to stay alive

They beckon me to join their cause
And get back in the game
I will someday, but my outlook
Will never be the same

I won't care if muscles ache
Or stubborn pounds won't go
Because I know how short the length
Of string on God's yo-yo

~K. Niebur

I am no longer afraid of death.

Ready Any Time

My friend and I who both had lost
Our partners missed so much
Confessed there's really nothing here
To match our loved one's touch

It's not that we have lost all joy
But if the truth were told
We're hoping we won't linger long
Won't have to grow too old

Some say that we're not moving on
Not reaching for the sun
Just walking dead and shuffling on
Until our lives are done

It's not that we have given up
Forgotten how to climb
It's just that we have come to know
We're ready any time

~K. Niebur

I know now, love is truly a gift...

Set it Free to Be

Neither of us may ever know
Why our paths had to blend
Of all the places we could be
God brought us near and then...

Nudged us close enough to touch
To love and share a kiss
Let us linger on and on
In warmth and light and bliss

I've learned to live so lightly now
Enjoying what may come
Treasure every sweet embrace
Until the time is done

I'll never question why again
When love comes finding me
I'll just give thanks with open heart
And set it free to be

~ K. Niebur

Will I remember how to fly?

Broken Bird

Each day I take my lonely heart
And hold it up to God
An aching bird with broken wings
Feet laden down with sod

With no hope of my own to cure
I say my daily prayer,
"Give me the strength to carry on
and wait for your repair."

Then let me stand on highest cliff
and have the faith to try
Toss my heart into the air
and trust that it will fly

~ K. Niebur

Grief through the Seasons

Grief through the Seasons

Just as your perspective changes, the seasons themselves, as reliable and repetitive as anything can be, take on a different quality. Tom and I always shared our enjoyment of the seasons, now I was experiencing them alone. I could no longer turn to him to comment on the colors of fall, the beautiful blankets of winter snow, the surprises of spring or the warmth of welcome summers. If I stood very still, though, in silent appreciation, I could almost feel him with me.

We see the cycle of life around us...
but expect to live forever...

Seasons

So life to death and back again
The seasons stay so true
We count on this but disbelieve
When comes to me and you

~K. Niebur

Some sadness is physical...

August's End (Fall)

You passed away at August's end
Just before the Fall
The trees put on their glory coats
And tried to fool us all

But soon they threw down all their leaves
To keep pace with my tears
And now my heart aches just like then
When comes this time of year

~K. Niebur

Some moments must still be shared...

As Snow grows Deep (Winter)

The snow keeps falling down and down
Puts blankets on your trees
And snow caps on your feeder tops
So cold, the winter's freeze

The snow drifts are God's winter beach
They shine up like white sand
Air crisp and clear stings cheeks to glow
And brings on winter's tan

I scatter seeds upon the ground
Your birds keep coming, still
I watch them from the warm inside
Pluck snow to get their fill

I wonder if you're watching me
Watch them as seeds they reap
They flit, they fly, I long to know
What winter beds they keep

I whisper up my thoughts to you
And wake eternal sleep
We stand together side by side
To watch as snow grows deep

~K. Niebur

Some sweet memories linger...

Every Drop of Rain (Spring)

Every drop of rain that falls
Lies glistening on the ground
Shining gems with worlds inside
Where trust and hope abound

All your trees drink hungrily
The streams of life thread 'round
Flowing to each branch and twig
Give birth without a sound

I watch each spring, as time goes on
God's silent song sent down
To sing in every drop of rain
Of all the love we found

My heart moves from its slumber then
Unfolding from its pain
Sweet memories cascading down
In every drop of rain

~K. Niebur

Some pains must be expressed...

The Memorial Garden (Summer)

I worked until sweat trickled down
I worked until I ached
I hacked and hoed and dug and plowed
And raged against our fate

I carved into the woods so dense
A clearing for the sun
And planted seeds and flowers and weeds
Until each day was done

I drug the piles of battered brush
Made bonfires to the sky
So I could singe God's feet, at least
For causing you to die

I yelled until I had no voice
Then fell down on my knees
Grabbed hands full of the dirt and rock
And threw them where I pleased

I knew, somehow, you'd understand
My need to punish earth
For swallowing your ashes down
Reclaim your gift of birth

When I was done, all bruised and spent
I saw what I had made
A garden full of bloom and life
Rimmed with fern and shade

I backed up to the garden bench
And eased down on the seat
Rested then my weary heart
And soaked up summer's heat

I knew that you'd be glad to see
That in my deepest pain
I planted still the seeds to grow
And counted on the rain

~K. Niebur

Acceptance

Acceptance

Acceptance of this kind of loss is more like an uneasy truce. It doesn't bring peace; it just ends the war. Your inner landscape is devastated. Old, trusted, structures lie in ruin inside you. You can't walk down any road without confronting your scars but you eventually give up trying to get 'back' to the way it was. You finally begin awakening each day ready – for how it is.

How comforting to know...
you really aren't alone...

Safe in the Grief

Go into the grief
And don't be afraid
For dark days, too
The Lord has made

You won't get lost
In this strange land
For God still has you
By the hand

He'll tend you there
Until you're done
Then walk you back
Into the sun

~K. Niebur

You never really get over it..

Grief is not tidy

Grief is not tidy
Grief is not linear
Bid farewell at breakfast
It comes back for dinner

It cries in its sleep
Awakens at two
Wanders into your bed
To curl up with you

It tosses and turns
It steals all the covers
It wanders the halls
It lingers and hovers

It flickers the lights
Adjusts the T.V.
A mischievous sprite
It won't let you be

But given its time
And given its due
It will find its place
And make peace with you

~ K. Niebur

And you are ambushed sometimes...

Pockets of Pain

Two years later
doing something as innocuous
as cleaning out a drawer
I touched the records of our life together
I saw your handwriting…
and felt the wave growing
At first, I resisted
No, please, I don't want to feel this
it's just a pocket of pain
I can ride it out, I can surf this
then I simply sank and let the wave flow over me
I placed my face in my hands and cried and cried

Later, I wondered how I ever survived the early weeks
when these waves were tidal and never-ending
that is the thing of it – the way God made us
to keep going
until we only stumble upon these pockets of pain,
fall into a wind tunnel of memories
that rip at our core…
makes us cry…
beg for mercy…
Then catch our breath…
and go on walking

~K. Niebur

If I could only carry a tune...
Perhaps a musician will see this
and help me put it to music

Think of You

(a song)

Is it really true?
All I have to do
Is think of you
Then you'll be right by my side
To hold me through the night
And all I have to do
Is think of you

Every day since you've been gone
I've had to try my best to go on
Struggling through the waves of pain
Wanting just to see you again
Now all I have to
Is think of you.

All I have to do
Is think of you
Then you'll be right by my side
To hold me through the night
And all I have to do
Is think of you

Can it be that love prevails
When everything else fails?
Reaching beyond time and space
To bring us to one place?
And all I have to do
Is think of you?

Is it really true?
All I have to do
Is think of you

Then you'll be right by my side
To hold me through the night
And all I have to do
Is think of you

Now I know we'll both go on
And I can still be strong
Sending all my love to you
Like a wave to carry us through
And all I have to do
Is think of you.

Yes, it's really true
All I have to do
Is think of you
Then you'll be right by my side
To hold me through the night
And all I have to do
Is think of you

~ K.Niebur

Bringing Him Forward

Bringing Him Forward

There was a speaker at the grief support group I attended who suggested we continue our relationship with our departed loved one by finding something special about them to incorporate into our lives – to take one of their 'causes' and make it our own. Tom had installed several bluebird houses in our fields. We would take walks to check them, peeking into the doors to count the eggs or watch the fat little babies crowd each other in the nest.

I decided to make bluebird houses for Tom's family and the project quickly blossomed. I ended up making 40 bird houses. As I constructed them, tears would fall but it felt so good to make something tangible in his memory. In this way, I could begin to 'go on' without leaving Tom behind. I brought him forward with me and for everyone who lovingly placed one of his bird houses in their yards.

My math may be faulty..
but I know he appreciates
my effort..

Bird House Math

One bird house plus mama and papa birds
Equals two nestings of 3 eggs each year
Forty houses, then equals 240 more birds in one year
Over ten years, then,
those forty houses can produce 2,400 more birds

But, there's more!
If all of the hatchlings find places to nest each year
and reproduce at a consistent rate
(and assuming an equal division of the population
into male and female birds),
then, in 10 years, there would be 1,574,640 new birds.

That's a lot of birds, honey.

You're welcome.

~K. Niebur

How freeing to know...
you don't have to 'go on'
without them...

Bringing you Forward

To leave you behind, brought too high a cost
We kept going back for something we'd lost
So we carry you forward, your family and friends
Alive in our hearts 'till we see you again

We hope you don't mind, we've borrowed from you
When we see with our eyes, we use your eyes, too
When looking for answers, we find them from you
And when your birds soar, our hearts ride with you

Stay happy. We're fine, made stronger it's true
As we tend all the things so important to you
We carry you forward, your family and friends
Alive in our hearts 'till we see you again

~K. Niebur

How wonderful to know...
they can truly still live inside you...

Now

Now you send me birds that sing
Butterflies with painted wings
Unwrapped gifts to catch my eye
And draw my heart into the sky

Love soars and glides upon the wind
Easy, free, to garner again
A seed of hope to grow a dream
Washed by rain to make it gleam

My soul soaks up the warmth of sun
Turning and turning to a life begun
With you, in me, brought home somehow
To live again in the joy of now

~ K. Niebur

In Memory

In Memory
of The Niedre's

In October of 2005, our small town was rocked by the murder of a particularly beloved couple. It was shocking that it could happen in our town, in broad daylight and even more shocking that the murderer was their own son. It affected us deeply and left so many unanswered questions. The only thing merciful I could find in the event was that they had died together and would not have to experience grief. I offer this poem in their memory.

The Innocent

(to the Niedre's)

The mystery can't be explained
The moment can't reveal
Lost ways, dead ends that roiled in pain
The wounds too deep to heal

To cause the hand to lift the gun
Like someone else's arm
Their very own and cherished son
The one to bring them harm

But bonded, blessed they had to be
To face together death
They passed on to eternity
And shared their life's last breath

Where past God's gate they realized
True mercy had been shown
And neither one would feel the pain
Of living on alone

So tragedies and mercy link
In some divine intent
To leave us with the unexplained
Yet shield the innocent

~ God bless you and keep you, K. Niebur

Author's Notes for
Widows and Widowers

Getting Help – My Biased Opinion

Find a group and
actively manage your grief.

My hat is off to people who can grieve stoically on their own and make it through in one piece. Most of us need some kind of help. I don't see individual therapy as the single best answer. A therapist may not have necessarily 'been there', even if they are trained in grief counseling. You need to be in the company of others who really do understand because they have been there or are there now. The fact is, grief **hurts**. *You can't really escape the pain and you can't be 'cured'. You have to find a way to survive it and live with it.*

Support Groups   *I was lucky enough to find a grief support group in my town that met each week. Its purpose was, and still is, to educate and to support people through the grief process. The experience is surrounded with myths and misstatements and causes things you probably never even heard of or expected. How about sleeplessness, memory loss, disorientation, indecision, random physical symptoms? These things can be frightening if left unexplained. Your loved one, intimacy, joy, companionship, your old life, yourself, your heart, your soul, your bearings, your sleep, your purpose, your role – all go missing for a time during grief. Having a place to go every week to spend time with others who are also missing these things is an indescribable comfort. In their company, I didn't need to explain anything. I could weep, or not; share a feeling or not, talk or just listen. Although everyone grieves differently, I found many, many feelings were common. You may feel abandoned, lonely, irritable, fear, panic, dread, anger, rage, relief... Had I not learned about those feelings from other people who really knew – I would have been constantly blindsided by the effects of grief and probably would have thought I was going insane.*

Finding a group isn't too difficult. Most funeral homes have contacts with groups in the area and with counselors who specialize in grief therapy. Hospice services are an excellent resource for finding groups. Some groups meet only for a few weeks; others meet weekly on an ongoing basis so it doesn't matter where you 'jump in' on the sessions.

If you can, find a group that suits you and, by all means, feel free to attend more than one group. You will find great comfort and healing there.

Writing Writing helps somehow, too. It gets your emotions described, out of yourself onto paper. Try writing your 'story' – the story of how you met, loved and lost your partner. When you have described a beginning, a middle, and an end to this particular chapter in your life, healing is encouraged. Even if your 'chapter' took up decades, most of your entire life, it is still a chapter with a beginning, a middle and an end. You are still here and have more chapters ahead – maybe none as wonderful, maybe none that will ever match the great chapter you wrote with your loved one. But your life isn't over. Coping is a long phase, healing a longer phase, creating new chapters is the transition into health and a life begun anew. Do what it takes, but 'do' is the operative word. Get involved with your own journey through this process. At times, the grief rolls you over and over as if you were in the grip of a deadly undertow but if you know how to ride it instead of fight it, you'll resurface and breathe again. Don't let it tumble you endlessly.

Reading Reading books about coping with grief can help, but the less technical and shorter books are probably more effective than lengthy, scholarly references. I've included a short list of books I personally found helpful. One, in particular, is similar to having a grief support group in a book. It was written by the leader of the grief group I attended, Marty McNunn. The name of the book is "A Group I Never Wanted to Join". It's brief, practical and includes the 'stories' of real people who experienced real loss and survived. You'll find yourself in there somewhere because people like you wrote these stories.

Whatever path of healing you take, good luck with your journey through grief.

~ Katherine Niebur

Recommended
Reading and Resources

Recommended Reading and Resources

Childs-Gowell, Elaine, A.R.N.P., Ph.D. _Good Grief Rituals – Tools for Healing_. New York: Station Hills Press. 1992. (Author's note: An interesting little book of active exercises and spiritual rituals to acknowledge and express your grief.)

Hickman, Martha Whitmore. _Healing After Loss – Daily Meditations for Working Through Grief_. New York: Avon Books, Inc. 1994. (Author's note: Short, daily readings. Very healing. My favorite everyday companion during the worst of my grief and beyond. I still pick this book up every few days to read and reflect.)

McNunn, Marty. _A Group I Never Wanted to Join – Practical Advice and Stories of Hope and Recovery for Grieving People_. Minnesota: Syren Book Company. 2005. (Author's note: Like a grief group in a book. Full of real stories of all types of losses from everyday people.)

Winston, Lolly. _Good Grief: A Novel_. Warner Books. 2004 (Author's note: This is fiction but could easily be reality. A moving story centered around a woman dealing with the loss of her husband. Told with humor and compassion.)

www.thegriefblog.com – Learn. Cope. Share. Heal. A division of the Open to Hope Foundation. (Author's note: This website is truly a gift to griever's everywhere. Informative and full of advice, poetry, stories, sharing; it's all there.)